# Re:Vision

Re:Vision
Re:Vision

# Re:Vision

Isi Unikowski

First published in 2025
Published by Puncher and Wattmann
PO Box 279
Waratah NSW 2298

https://www.puncherandwattmann.com
web@puncherandwattmann.com

ISBN 9781923099418

Cover image: Clarice Beckett (c1927) *October morning*, Gift of Alastair Hunter OAM and the late Tom Hunter in memory of Elizabeth through the Art Gallery of South Australia Foundation 2019, Art Gallery of South Australia, Adelaide, 20197P100

Cover design by Isi Unikowski and David Musgrave
Typesetting by Morgan Arnett
Printed by Lightning Source International

A catalogue record for this work is available from the National Library of Australia

*For my mother Rachel and in memory of my father Jack*
*Alexander and Miriana*
*and especially for Lidia*

# Contents

# Pumping station

Bowler-hatted, unsmiling, moustachioed,
a group of men stands beside the big machines.
Apprentices crouch, caps awry as their grins.
The manager's wife flaunts the region's first car.
In these huge posters by the ticket office,
it's easy to mistake the time the shutter took to descend
for gravitas, as if they were watching us.

Once inside, the polished, gleaming semi-darkness makes
the glare barricaded at the entrance look cheap and flat.
Huge pistons are poised, about to resume
their genuflections, giant flywheels stationary beside them
as though the parts of some celestial clockwork
had been dismantled and lined up.

The guide balances a coin on the casing
to show how smoothly the piston rods perform,
without the least vibration, in greased silence.
Our kids, from a world of few moving parts,
where whatever machinery is left
is so well-hidden it might as well be magic,
go back outside for better reception, unimpressed.

But I linger out of curiosity:
for all the size of these components,
there was an amenable logic
and purpose to the way rocking beams, cranks, rods
moved and pulled and pushed, visibly connecting
to the task or purpose

of lifting and conveying the most basic elements of a city
from one place to a much better place

and nostalgia too, for the reticent confidence
in machinery tooled with such precision,
yet still decorated, made beautiful in filigree and ornament
as though sludge had its sacral moments too
for all the boilers' black, bulky
indestructibility; to make a machine
that could operate with such grace

as if all that was needed to keep the world in motion
was someone in overalls proudly standing by
with a little can of oil.

# A seashell

Black rocks exposed by the low tide seem to have drawn
into themselves all sunlight and spindrift, concealed
any promise of pails and castles amongst their pockmarks.

The horizon is burred as a badly honed blade,
bleak as my replies
despite which she tramps along, asking only
to walk closer to the water where the sand is firmer, reminded
of her childhood holidays on the cold shores of the North Sea,
entrusted by her parents to careful boarding-house routines.

Yet what happened yesterday
has been sucked under a languid mat of floating fronds
that trails us the length of our walk.  We pause
to watch toddlers and their mothers,
intent on the weekday freedom of the beach.

Days later, I find a shell that she must have picked up,
secreted in the glovebox and forgotten; with a child's pleasure,
she would have hurriedly rinsed it before I'd notice,
a common scallop shell, dry docked
among the holed turrets and bitten limpets
marking out the tide line

its red ridges half covered by a calciferous impasto,
white plaster slathered over the base,
polystyrene sea-foam frozen in its concave basin,
as if the little creature within
had drawn up a genie's pantaloons for decorum.

Scornfully, I almost toss it out: of all the shells on that beach,
she had to pick such a disappointing specimen, that so fails
to show the shape and colour of which *Pecten fumatus* is capable
that offers such a sardonic, such a *redundant* symbol.

Yet something of her chuckle at the naughty boys
who scared and fascinated her brief adolescence
prompts me to relinquish all comparison
between this example of its kind and all the others,
significance sufficient in being chosen.

So I have kept the shell here on a shelf
where it may outlive us both in a hereafter
that might have been better served on a beach

to do its time: perhaps as shelter
for some passing shore crab
then shard, then grit,
then a bracelet of minerals for the wind.

# The last of summer

Heat arrives from over the Brindabellas
as though they're the lip of a basin pouring sunset
down the Cotter Road; heat like old quarrels
that have flickered to life, chafe of crowds
rubbing each other up the wrong way,
earth-anger, quicklime kiln-ditches,
artillery from distant wars
putting the heat on oblivious cities, racing towards
ember-struck villages beyond negotiation,
making it hard to sleep.
          Now that I've put my glasses on the bedside table,
all I can see, from the corner of my eye,
are two hands, fluttering like a pair of birds.
I don't know who this cheerful woman is
or what she's telling my wife watching her on YouTube
propped up late under earphones. The woman seems to be pointing
this way and that, her polished, bright red fingernails
and animated smile a match with the borders
of fabrics she holds up, jiggling, making them do
a little dance before she lays them down again,
gestures like a shopkeeper inviting you
to examine a fine bolt.
          Heat like the big bang pressed between
the blank pages of Genesis: one moment
there's nothing; the next it's all there, a scrawl
of lightning, a word packing heat, and suddenly
there are skies, seas, birds, a moon,
a helpmate wanded from a rib,
a story that tells it all wrong

presses out hope in its mangle
because it says nothing of technique, art that compels
measurement, cutting-out, a pattern, pins and weights,
an art infatuated by the textile it holds,
celebrating its slipperiness, thickness, flimsiness
its awkward dimensions, its ornery creases and folds
stubborn abutments, puckered seams,
the needle's free will and breakage
all hailed in the design, held by the maker's intent
as she celebrates the conjunction of two shapes
that would be hard to line up if it weren't for a method
she learned from a friend, from her mother,
or as here from a stranger. That, too,
is where the old yarn has it wrong,
because what is created here is never created
alone: deep histories confided in the aisles
between ticking, duck and batting,
no sooner learned than conveyed,
the binding that prevents life from fraying,
solidarity in the endeavour
established by a stranger's advice, an admiring remark
as the assistant measures out a purchase.
After an ad for buttons
the woman seems to be finishing up; a quilt
will soon be complete, turned for display
like mist beginning to drift across the ranges
to reveal early snow, a scatter of mussed threads
stitching the high firetrails together

and I finally fall asleep.

# Collecting

The weatherboards built years earlier across the street were ex-Army:
the hard-drinking sergeant who'd have fistfights with his sons,
the captain who wept for grief when his own son joined up
for the rumblings and gauntlets he could expect,
the guy on the corner who used his huge Army knife
to skin rabbits, then hung their pelts on a wall in his garage; and their wives,
who queued at the bread van in curlers and housecoats
and, most astonishing of all, kept chewies and ciggies revolving
together around sitreps and local weather reports.
            But not once,
as I turned up on their porches and their screen doors squeaked open
to me holding a card with a space for their signatures,
its incomprehensible Old Testament script
about poor Jewish orphans
and a little plastic bag for coins,
not once in the streets of that suburb where my parents' ark
had come to rest, miles from where our Sunday School teachers
had expected we'd go out collecting,
not once was I ever received with words that lacerated,
with anything less than good cheer.  Even those who gave nothing
closed their doors with such a gentle regret
it seemed less refusal than deference
to the long, dark corridors of those little bungalows
to which they returned,
called back to the greater mystery of their sheds.

# ‘If I were called in to construct a religion’

— Philip Larkin

But no-one these days goes in much for constructing religions:
too many spivs padding about at the auctions, too dark in the alleys
away from the ferris wheel’s brilliant lights,
upturned shopping trolleys beside the gimcrack malls,
wonky castors insisting on their own directions.
Called in to account for faith in something, though,
I too would fix my footings in elements indifferent to our nature:
a callistemon’s redness beyond our need to know
what red is, what the bees dance into; a Manchurian pear
where it catches the first of autumn’s light; the sweetness
of that transition, plenitude sufficient
in the conversation between sun and shadow in its cells,
hibiscus that taunts the frost with its carnival
undaunted beyond all sanctions of the season.
If I have forgotten to celebrate the earth
let that be my error that I now confess.

# No, wait, really

*after 'Wait' by* Galway Kinnell

She comes to his office in such despair at the end
of a relationship he has to ask her not to do anything rash
but to return in the afternoon, when he pretends
he knows what he's going to say. It's a slapdash
answer to her problem and somewhat misses the point.
But, in the meantime, he has an appoint-

ment. The need to drop everything — such tedious
panel-beating of buckled grammar,
filling logical potholes in the curious
epistemology of the last-minute crammer,
smoothing the wrinkles from last year's lecture notes —
he assumes we'll take for granted; what he wrote

up later, in that piratical way poets perfect
of secreting someone else's hurt
on some unmapped, deserted prospect
of a page sounds so *useless* to him, so *old guy*, so curt
— standard 'everything will be all right' counterplot.
Well, what then? If not that, then what?

is what he sweats over all afternoon, pencil tucked
behind his ear; what he really wants is to share
his hope that she hears not some wisdom plucked
from the pages of his desk calendar; not even that someone cared
a little, but cared enough to put a line break *there*
between two stanzas, the repetition of certain words just where

they will have most effect; that she might discern
how the patience to make a whole line of that one imperative
might prove to be a guide through life's upturns and downturns.
And he doesn't hear the sound of someone's submissive
knocking. He doesn't hear, as his muttered revisions overscore
the urgency of someone knocking in the empty, darkening corridor.

# The Tidbinbilla Plates

*after* Fred Williams' *'Sherbrooke' etchings*

*1. Grounding the plate*

Over familiar suburbs, the mountain's blue silhouette
clouds lowering their balloon gondolas onto its peak
little white faces of tourists peering down
at a precise grid of firetrails, fences, plantations
containing the strewn canopy.
A hawk patrols the mountainside's green hoarding.

Adam with a ranger's guide, I prepare by making the names
of ghost gum, scribbly gum and barrel gum strange
against my tongue. Dabbing at the plate
as if to cover earth beneath asphalt, wax and resin.

*2. A drawing is cut onto the plate*

A human thing, to want to know what that light is
that has followed me all my life, and now waits for me
to lay out gravers, make a groove, add another.
As I clear the detritus, light
advances in its trenches, as if to witness each incision
add ornament to the world.
Motion itself is the thought, every score
brings me a step closer to the forest
the lines I cut a stencil of what I have yet to see
a script I have yet to learn.

*3. The plate is dipped in acid*

moving words to their vanishing point.  Torn, abraded,
gaps on the plate. The mountain no longer visible in the west.

Mordant bites into memory, the drawn forest
degraded like cellulose film lost in the archives.

Where the plate reveals its face I'm given the remnants of bushfire,
wet eucalyptus bark, years mottled as mackerel skin.

The more the acid takes away, the less I control,
the less I know what I'm going to find there.

Names of things and people becoming elusive,
memory restricted to ritual, repeated actions. Plates rocking in their bath.

*4. The plate is inked*

from the Greek for 'burned in'.  I step back,
allow sunlight to enter a stand of dark saplings
as though I looked out, sight without frame
through rain compiling its index to the world.
Dark patches in pools where lines converge and cross,
Styx as Tube maps, explorers' voyages
traced in a school atlas.  Dark spice capillaries.
Ink runs darker from deeper cuts on the backs of slaves.
Memorial poles in shades of black and grey
showing absent nations their way back to the mountain.

*5. The plate passes through a press*

In the evening, I cut a forest in its image and after its likeness.
Rollers pressed above and below the plate; ink bled and feathered
in designs of faulty replication, each state degraded to its truth in my sight
as though there were a plan all along: first, receptacles of air, light, water, earth,
then animals, birds, completion of the sequence
as though this were the final state. But I watch
how acid's random, momentary action makes one thing
resemble another, while that demands resemblance of something else.
I wipe the plate clean and begin again, cutting
into morning light, sun rising into its silence.

# Funny accents and pickles

It begins with an aleph, the diminutive
only two people in the world know me by
so when they're gone, that me will vanish too,
as our *mishpOOcheh* –
the way we pronounce the Yiddish word for 'family'
that instantly identifies us as plebeian,
not a classy *mishpOche*–
and the people who speak to me in Yiddish
become fewer still, a fact that obliges me to avoid
*kintzen*, the word my folks use to dismiss gimmicks,
antics, superficial showiness,
whatever calls undue attention to itself
like those who say they speak this *mameloschen*
because they know two or three profanities
that would never be used by those
who made their home in it,
our gentle, kind teachers
who, before we knew what we must have meant to them,
tried so hard to get something into our *farshtopte kep*
when all we wanted was to be playing downball
against a brick wall that faced the street
in the shining Sunday morning, that boundless *in drawsen!*
to which my Dad would expel my brother and me
when our wrestling scuffed the skirting boards.
Too busy to find its own words for herbs that ignited passion,
doused a fever, wildflowers that tugged at the sides of village lanes,
Yiddish trudged from one place to another with its sack
that got heavier and bulkier with *breklech* from the world's table,
places that were home but never home

seen only in caricature:
funny accents, yokels carting pickles,
embarrassing relatives *krechtzen oy vey!* as they pinched kids' cheeks
from their couches in tenements of normality
behind which we fidgeted and forgot, *nebech,* that in Yiddish
a *khokhme*— the word for a joke —
is the same as the word for wisdom.

# Threads for the convent girls

*for Rachel*

We've got the place to ourselves, so it's easy to imagine
as we pause in light rising from display panes
that we have joined a bishop who has arrived
to inspect the girls' preparations for marriage
and for bringing the truth to the sullen forests of the north.
His cope spreads above us like the translucent wings
of a huge morning-beetle lifting out of the dew.
Hands behind our backs we wander like him
through newly painted galleries, over the polished parquetry.

Does he know the special benediction of young women's
laughter? Or is it stilled at his entry?
Having stood to greet him, the girls resume their work
their thin fingers, blotched with cold, reaching
for another bead.  They are never warm, these girls.
(They will never be warm.)

And does he know that angels are leaning over their shoulders
to watch them work, copying the push and tug
with which they fix silver and gold twists?
While the girls reach into a box for beads and threads
angels are reaching into the box for their future,
laying black threads of illness across a throat,
binding wrists in threads of fire and fever,
picking out threads white as rivers
that will carry them into the wilderness,
grey for the winters of a soul's seasons,
blue for the evenings of a husband's absence.

But I stop for a moment. Because it occurs to me
my mother was a convent girl too, for a while.
1942, Belgium. Hidden
with her sister and mother in an orphanage run by nuns.
One day (a day of gold threads)
my grandmother, returning from errands in a nearby town
was about to knock on the convent's front door,
not knowing that the Gestapo was on the other side
questioning the Mother Superior. Just at that moment,
someone she didn't recognise, a priest perhaps,
hurried past, beckoning for her to follow, away, to safety.

And that's the trouble with angels: they only exist if they're punctual.
Evanescent fibres of some unknown element,
they only linger if we remember not to break them
by stepping on the threads.

As we leave, we replace the pamphlets,
thank the student at reception,
hand you all back to your lives, follow sunshine
reflecting off the cobblestones outside
back out through the doors
as they are opened for us.

# The man who spoke playground

Just there on the rise, before the road descends
into older suburbs on one side, where new estates
have replaced the pine forest where the kids once
threw sticks into a creek now turned into a street name,
my daughter and I have come to a small playground.
Above us a shade sail, like the wing
of a huge raptor tethered to creosote-dark posts,
strains toward the Brindabellas
as if casting the shadow of a cloud on their side.

Why does the mention of *Antrim Road*
seem to evoke so much more than
the name of the road that runs past us here?
Famine and dispersal, certainly, even when viewed
from so far away, the way so much of Canberra lies
compact below us, lending itself to such speculation.
Does that mean such resonance can't be summoned?
Can *Cotter Road* never be given the shape in your mouth
that *Raglan Road* takes in mine?
    (After all, Cotter was an Irish settler; and 'Antrim' means 'a ridge').

Howls from the RSPCA's kennels,
as if Dante's Inferno lies just behind the Maccas over there,
suggest not, suggest
I come back to now, come back
to the equipment pearled in frost, the swing's
slight movement from the wind's touch, or perhaps
my daughter kicking off in distraction,
the ranges' lilac cummerbund in the distance.

The shade sail above us points to rain drifting in
along the river corridor, over the observatory that squats on its hill,
over the glowing brake lights of miniature concrete trucks
heading to the outskirts, over days
that run like a film coming to spool's end when they're happy,
or turned over one by one like photos in an album when they're not,
over this place graced by a name without resonance,
only by time passing
with the sound of a magpie's wing
cutting the face of a diamond
from the morning's cold quiet.

## ‘There’s some mighty good water in Tennessee’

*Abraham Lincoln’s advice as defence attorney to an abused woman on trial for murdering her husband in self-defence, whereupon she absconded and was not pursued further.*

Tonight, America, the stars above you have been blotted out
by flitting shapes, like huge moths attracted
to haloes of darkness that form around pools
of doubt, smutches of innuendo, whispered
confidences in bars; the more implausible, the deeper
the ravines cut by these rivers of pitch,
the more their deltas entice, glossy as onyx.
So they have come from afar to look at you, America,
and now their gauzy drift settles
over the islands of Puget and Penobscot,
scrimlight of your ordinary evenings dimmed
beneath their feathered jostling.

And why not? Haven’t you earned some portent
to mark these times? Shouldn’t huge storm-clouds be rushing
to pound like breakers on the reef of your cities, Joshua trees
uncannily bursting into flame beside littered highways,
flattened corn like notes in a Sousa requiem for an empire?

> (—here, where the purple light of Canberra’s dusk
> fills this room at the back of the house
> my regrets won’t stir a blade of your prairie grass
> even as they form around your name —)

*America* where Hart Crane came ashore,
where I linger on a corner while Stevens pauses to write
something on an envelope; I wave at Berryman drinking
alone in Hopper's bar. *America* was an intricate
machine, a timing light shone
into the engine well of neighbourhoods and precincts,
an inscribed disk sent into the future.

*America* from where my brother and I would emerge
to walk home from the little local cinema.
You turned the real world into plywood,
a papier-mâché bricolage plastered over
the cold late afternoon. *America*
the stories you told about yourself in technicolour
bore a fidelity to the colours of another reality
not ours, a soundtrack out of sync
with the words we spoke.

America, your pure products address you.
They declaim from the commerce on your riverbanks,
from your deserted promontories,
from your heartland constructed like a filmset
in a language scattered
and capacious, its talismans stashed in mangroves and malls,
beacons off the bluff, the cape,
your resonant shores; no hamlet so mean,
so forgotten off a byway it will not have its place
in your intonations of highways and lakes.

(— not you, not here, say the cockatoos
their call like straps of darkness tightening.
The reticence of our drawl
stretches like an ill-fitted sheet to its continent
unless we too are located by names
that move like windlight through the casuarinas —)

Tonight, I'm thinking of what *America* meant
to the camp inmates like my Dad, crowded around a window, April 1945.
They asked the ones who could look out
'can you see them, the Americans? Can you see them yet?' and when
they arrived, the Sixth Armored Division, when they entered
the camp, how amazed he was, my Dad, still a teenager,
who had never seen an American.

America, I'm thinking too about that accused woman.
How perhaps, in her last years, she found deep wells of that fine water
in Tennessee. About the angels that she found there.

# An angel is waiting behind every wall

i

In the oldest part of the ancient city, people are stuffing bits of paper into the crevices between the huge blocks of a wall. On the paper are written prayers, requests, invocations. Then some of them wipe their eyes, head home to wives unable to conceive, delinquent sons, husbands who stare at them as though they were pages torn from a prayer book. On the other side of the wall, angels file the petitions. On those considered to have accurately appraised the situation the angels write '*OK for processing*'; on others that have not, '*new draft required*'. Only a few messages are ever lost. These somehow meander back through the cracks, back between the blocks, back to where they are whisked up into the sky by the breeze that plays in a corner of the square before the wall and distributes them in envelopes marked '*Pigeon*'.

ii

A dishevelled day: the vast station was teeming with workers and students returning for the holidays, and we were propelled through the wrong exit to where some youths, posing as guides, scooped us into a van and promptly got lost themselves. They deposited us at the gardens but at the wrong entrance where a guard, surprised by our sudden appearance, stood agape as we scurried in. We followed paths the guide book promised would bring us to a renowned imperial relic, a wall so old (the guidebook said), it could no longer be seen apart from the trees that had grown from its bricks and crenellations. But we were following the paths backwards, and so wandered further away to the wrong side of the park. Nevertheless, we found a wall. *Here it is!* we told ourselves. It seemed old and mossy enough. Musing dutifully in front of it, we tried to feel what six hundred years was meant to feel like. Birds rustled among the lianas that had grown over it, and I could hear palm leaves rustling in the warm breeze, as though the angel of history were rubbing his wings together, like a miser.

## Handwriting remembered

as hull-kiss        keel-glide        sea-foam cursive

as plastic dipping-pens with cork grips and a blue callus on the middle
    finger

as the hand repeating what was first heard in the mind

as the need to take care with words that, once formed,
could not be taken back, only hidden
behind sapphire and graphite foliage

so that the paper thinned and sometimes tore beneath
strokes of dismissal, propped sticks of insertion
proclaiming the superiority of a new word
perched above the scribble (that word barely remembering
how it began in the word for 'cut'
as it was said by people who never
wrote on the steppes' ruled lines)

as my southpaw knuckles were struck
to make me write with the other hand,
the one that, perfecting, didn't seek a better word,
but learned to hold three pens at a time
so that it was easier to write out
'I must not use my left hand
I must not use my left hand
I must not use my left hand'

as the ache of disuse, the wrist-shackle
that now accompanies a shopping list,
allows the ‘e’ to close, the ‘f’ to curl inwards
as if resigned to its punishment:
I must not use my left hand
I must not use my least hand
I must not lose my lost hand.

# The Museum of Unmet Expectations

How discreetly birds must die elsewhere!
Here, the entrance is littered with tiny carcasses,
beaks up, as if the sun were some last, huge seed
    of epiphany.

On street corners outside, laughter's a kind of currency.
But as you pass, the moneychangers go *tsk*
derisively, thumbs stationary,
    as if affronted.

Once inside, the quiet reminds you
of cavernous antiques stores in country towns.
Sickly grey squares all that's left on the walls,
    so labels make do

for the awkward few shuffling in from the provinces,
too sheepish to rise to the tour guide's provocations.
A guard texts surreptitiously
    to fill in the hours.

A group of schoolkids points to a diorama
that shows a chiming forest, and a tribe that mourns
downtime, the way other tribes grieve during
    a solar eclipse.

They have no expectation
that as their screens darken, their kin will reappear.
They're turning off the lights in the long galleries. Loot
    from sundered empires

has been packed away,
embroidered platitudes pricked into samplers
by girls with ruined eyesight grow mouldy
            in the damp basement.

So you join the families picnicking by the exit,
kneel with them on rugs
to dispense fairy bread to children who nibble, then spark
            off across the lawn

like sub-atomic particles in trajectories of joy
midday's squat shadows mimicking shrieks and laughter.
And when the kids have gone, you stare after them,
            over their heads

into the distance, the way people do on the news
when they are trying hard
to focus on a reporter's questions. As if after a great storm.
                        As if after fire.

# A bag of pinwheel biscuits

The local cakeshops were not *ethnic* enough for us
with their glutinous lemon tartlets,
precise demarcations of vanilla slices,
Neenish tarts and layer cakes,
lamingtons stacked like miniature railway sleepers,
lascivious eclairs and cream buns,
glacé cherries, sugared flowers and pearls,
rows of pink and green meringues arrayed on glass shelves,
slightly puzzling tokens of passage between
that world and ours.
        But there was a little shop where, sometimes,
on the way home from Sunday School, we'd stop to buy
a paper bag's worth of chocolate pinwheel biscuits,
their warmth leaving a dark slick on the paper.
And then there was my grandmother's famous *lekach*,
an almond flour cake that had to wait for my pronouncement
when, to everyone's jovial expectation,
I would be invited not to taste, but to hold
a slice close to my ear and squeeze,
reporting on its satisfactory hiss, like a receding wave,
ingredients settling in amicable proportion,
a sheen on my fingers lifted to my ears, with every slight press
hearing "this is how it was,
and then this, and then this..."
learning that taste alone
makes a poor judge of risen things
that can be sliced too thickly,
that sometimes have burnt edges,
and sometimes, like the tiny centre of a chocolate swirl

pressed onto a plate, left too long,
begin to grow hard and dry.

# An olive tree in flower

A B-grade movie drumbeat of doors and panes,
all night the wind tackles this eyrie
where I will try to sleep on the sofa-bed that only I have mastered
beneath photos of great-great grandmothers in *sheitels*,
graduations, weddings, and someone who looks like me
leaning against a first car.

My hollow-eyed cave-wall reflection presides over
the empty intersection below. Streetlight touches
a bag of cherries growing pulpy, a newspaper creased at the obituaries,
the Ezi-Read calendar floating in the darkened kitchen.
Dishes gleam where Dad sang as he did the washing up,
motes rising in staves of moonlight as if the melody lingered.

They waited hopefully all day for one of my famous jokes.
But my humours bubbled away in solicitude's alembic,
all day my tempers hissed and leaked
like a geothermal zone, bubbles of impatience popping
as my dogged, dutiful performance was transformed
into fairy-tale kindness in chats with the neighbours,

conversations gapped by what they mustn't be told
about family crises, dispatches from distant wars
and on the other side of telling,
the names of villages and cameo players' stories
scattered like pages from albums
as the binder's glue crumbles.

A last look at my e-mails.  My wife has sent me
a picture of our olive tree. To her delight
it has flowered for the first time,
a smattering of white and green neon bunting,
nubs askew, like families holding hands in kindergarten paintings.
Perhaps after fruitless years pot-bound roots have found
a way through to the soil,

or perhaps
it was time for some fabled bird,
down from circling time's thermals, high and alone,
to lift its flamboyant tail from the garden's tapestry
into a momentary renown.

# Cleaning windows

You're working hard, mate, but you don't labour well.
(If bad workers blame their tools, good ones choose more wisely.)
You hold the corners of those cloths as though they were the golden
fleece

but that won't do. To see best into the world,
to blur the balk, carom and careen beyond,
you first need to find rags of good cotton, their high thread count

an imprint of how those who lay under the sheets
they've been cut from lived; how they talked to one another
in the darkness, waited for dawn, cried out in dreams or love.

You need to focus on specks of grit blown in
from dry-spittle pasturelands; spider webs, bird shit, rain
patterning the void, children's fingerprints where they tried to touch
what they saw.

Then you have to rub the pane hard enough to make
the glass sing of the sand from which it came, the heat
that passes through it from the sun that it holds

and gives back. Listen for that sound to tell you
how the world you're pining for outside was poured like glass,
floated above the bed of its passing, spread into its frames,

how the very word '*glass*' flows
from a word so far back it's neither solid nor liquid
but we're told once meant '*to shine*'.

# Coming back

When we found our way back to what used to be our home

lanes still meandered from the church,
mud and weeds softening their sides,
water still collecting in the ruts
clouds lugging that blue sky
like workers carrying a new window
            it was all still the same

the sign over the shop on the corner still said
'milk and bread', urns were still stacked on the side
there was still a little chair by the entrance
where the owner could sit when things were quiet
while flies dozed on the window ledge
            they could even have been the same flies

in a yard somewhere, as always a child was yelling
whether in play or anger, until cut off
by an angry word from inside, admonished by
the silence that followed, the silence of a whole village listening
            it was all still the same

there was still copperplate in chalk on the blackboard
at the school, we could still find our initials
carved into the desk tops that our teachers occasionally used
to knock some facts into us
            amazing how it was all still the same

and the fence still leaned as if to catch
a passer-by's gossip; and smiled at what it heard
through its missing palings
        and that was still the same, too

and our house was still there, I recognised its stucco façade
untouched, the parlour at the front
as if we could have just walked in the front door
and climbed the narrow stairs up to the bedrooms

from where a stranger leaned out over the rug she was beating
and shouted '*Bugger off!*'
at us, and then again as we looked up, startled
'*Bugger off back to where you came from!*'
slammed the window down hard

        and the village went all quiet again

# The half-car to Once

In a quiet corner of the grounds, beyond the path's last turn,
an old car was set up for the patients with dementia. Its dash was restored,
dials, gears, ignition,
as though this car — at least, the front half — was ready to tour
the local countryside. For a treat
they'd bring someone out, put them on the torn bench seat

give them the keys, let them linger as they dreamt of driving to wherever. Home, mostly.
Not the last one, the one they left for here. Those who lived there, that house, all gone,
buried beneath ghostly
freeways of the recent past. There are more important roads they need to be on.
Mum and Dad waiting for their weekly visit, the roast
already carved and cooling beside the gravy in its boat.

And he could save himself and his wife-to-be the tack
of wasted years, if he could only find the courage
to explain he has to leave early to meet a girlfriend in a deserted cul-de-sac
between the oval's lopsided hockey goal and the colleges
from where they will drive to the squally beach, a general store
and her beside him, looking at dunes of pigface and spinifex, before

it turns into a suburb of couch grass and barbecues. Someone
is off to their family *dacha*, 90 versts from Moscow.

Every visitor is welcome to come in, it's their place, after all! The
samovar is on,
while the driver rests from the journey, sprawled on that couch with
the throw
(which turns out to be, to everyone's alarm, a distressed old lady's
rail-corralled bed.). Daughters open curtains to reveal shady

avenues leading up to patios. The half-car's journey always leads
to a body's uniquely-shaped place, the one destination that brightens
the past. There is no traffic on these roads to constrict and frighten,
no roadworks embody strangers' voices.
Tendons exult as they pull the stick shift; palsied hands turn keys.
As they remember a skill performed, thin limbs awaken and rejoice.

# Origins of the empirical method

One day, Galileo climbs to the top of the tower from where he addresses his students
as they gaze at him from below: 'Now watch,' he calls down at them,
'My left hand holds a miniature day in glass: a row of houses,
between them a street down which an old man walks,
children skating, people shovelling coal, a servant washing clothes.
On my right, a cannon ball found below the city walls
its dark surface blistered and cratered as though every siege had left its mark.
When I let them go, what difference will there be between them?'

But he's not satisfied with their guesses, so he says, 'Pay attention:
In one hand, I'm holding a raindrop. It reflects the sun's passage
across the blue vaults above as if inscribed in silver. In the other hand
is a teardrop I took from the eye of a corpse
we have kept for our students in the university's department of anatomy.
Opaque as chalcedony, it holds neither joy nor sadness.
Divested of its purpose it no longer shines with hopes or memories.
When I open my hands, what difference can you see between them?'

Now there is general consternation in the little group below
and even some vituperation between scientific factions as they form.
Troubled and dispirited, Galileo descends from the tower.
He glares at the students, first from his left eye, then from his right.
'With this telescope', he says, 'I see the moon waver and swing in its path, I pierce
the veils that surround Venus. And with my spectacles, I can read
the fine print in the letters of indictment and sentence against me.
Which lenses would you say are more powerful?'

But by this time, however, no-one's answering and no-one's guessing.
Having found the demonstrations perplexing, the students are drifting away
to a popular bar in the centre of Pisa where, under the awnings,
they are enjoying their beers while watching snow-flakes fall,
and their teacher as he packs away the glass sphere, the cannon ball,
the raindrop, the tear, his telescope and his spectacles.
'And yet they're still moving!' he mutters defiantly, though which object he means
by this is unclear, as no-one has stayed to take lecture notes.

# Fricatives of the Western Wood Peewee

*our chief need is for ornithologists to start talking about the facts of bird sound in an agreed-upon language*
— Richard Hunt, *1927*

Tested and rehearsed, what he hears is lost
in translations from an impossible language.
*'Gone beyond the limits of practicability'*
it's said of his system, briefly mentioned
for a year or two before it vanishes, dismissed,
leaving him still taking dictation from these beings
in their human-like speech; predictable, unreliable
dispatches from their leafy domains,
guardians of the perimeters between the bright uplands.
'Maniacal', 'tremulous', 'lusty' he scribbles.
Capture by capture, he knows he has interrupted
and limited the story they're telling, deciding
which of them should be heard, speak, or sing.
Whose talk is being emulated? he wonders, yet perseveres
with translation's reticent etiquette
his pen putting down 'bombinate', 'flump', 'lispering',
when what he wants to say is *'jealous'*, *'capricious'*, *'swift-footed'*.

# A parapet for the roof

*mostly illogical imperatives, prohibitions and rigorous modes of existence*
— CK Williams

I suppose my mother's gesticulations from the women's gallery
on the Day of Atonement, surreptitious eating motions
at my brother and me that meant it was time
for a visit to our car (prudently stationed blocks away),
weren't as apparent to everyone else as they seemed to us,
though surely, we cringed,
the entire congregation must have noticed
her invitation to transgress?

And every year, the same debate:
whether the cup of wine should be raised or lowered
just at that point in the *seder*,
a word meaning 'order,'
a challenge to our lack of certainty
as the children instructed their grandfathers
on what needed to be properly done.

Now I have lost the gift of repetition
I can no longer see these husks
produce their garlands of variation.

And if once I saw a man weeping in that congregation
so that someone set a chair aside for him —
angrily mistaking my childish, unguarded fascination for mockery —
I know enough now to know

that when someone weeps like that
it's kindest to leave them
to what all ritual freely chosen bestows:
a separate place that compresses place,
a time that foreshortens time,
a broken pattern, opened sky
for the soul we had almost forgotten,
the life we almost lived, to unfurl.

Doing the washing-up, for instance: no more now
than an occasion to brood,
the glasses' rims a tiara of offences taken
while Dad, on the other hand, sings his favourite bits from the liturgy,
as he handles each dish slowly, as if it were an offering:
repeated, lifted, adorned
in opalescent suds.

# Newton's Cradle

I know that there will be a night when we
will lie like this together for the last time.
If it should be years from now
it would still have come too soon.
But should it be tonight,
if tonight some inattentive or distracted cell
should plough wantonly
through the busiest cardiac intersection,
drive the wrong way down a one-way synapse,
belief is not enough to hold me
in the blue and red flashing lights of henceforth.
If it must be tonight
only by the indifference of science
am I reassured that the first law of love can be proven,
in the manner of a high school science teacher
who knows that the class is lost to him
(they have turned from him toward a world that beckons
through small screens and large windows)
yet still is forced by their beauty
to proclaim equations on a grimy whiteboard
for the wave that taps through spheres knocking on his desk
the way my shocked soul —
in its sudden check and backward arch
like a crash dummy stopped, slapped against
the test wall, the ballooning bag
— will be propelled forever forward
into your future, love remaining love
when it most alteration finds.
And so I begin my psalm, my chorus,

I too must write my equations on the whiteboard:
*'the conservation of love is given by the following statement...'*

# After Troy

The Odyssey Book XXV*

That night, after the gods had counselled peace
and the combatants had put away their armour,
Odysseus wandered through the streets of Ithaka. He strolled past
the strip bar spruikers, garish fast food stores,
astonished at how it had changed in his absence.
Half-visored in sweat and the light from a neon Coke sign,
he could hear the crowd around him laughing above
the fountains' hiss, then pooling in silence around some kid
playing flamenco, the god beside him listening too,
her face, huge as a suburb, so low and near
he could feel her breath in the streetlights.

Odysseus recognized her, and complained bitterly:
You who gives us war and reason, he asked,
why, of all those who fought, why
was I alone unable to return for so long?
The city we destroyed seems more familiar
than the streets I grew up in; and as that smoking plain receded
no-one on board could remember why the war had begun.
We forgot who was besieged and who had besieged them.
And having won, we no longer had to remember
the cause of our quarrel as we quarrelled amongst ourselves.

And the god answered him
*On my orders we ask them to travel great distances*
*military plans are robust*
*a new and different war for the protection*

*of our people and our way of life*
*a conflict so complex and heart wrenching*
*no simple act of revenge. It is no knee-jerk response*
*to meet the common danger in accordance with our constitutional*
*processes*
*we had compliments from all the participants about our soldiers*

Then Odysseus said to her
The task you gave us carried us over the breakers
of frost that fringed our blankets as we lay in the sand.
You gave us a curse, a cause, you were our reason
for leaving, our craft. We listened, mastbound, to your stories,
you made us forget in our laughter not even the gods
had missed us at the rites. Now when I read what they say
about us, when I watch some footage showing us on patrol
out beyond the wire, evening falling like porchlight
on the mountains of Uruzgan, I see my comrades,
once so familiar, truculent at first turn taciturn.
Something boar-like stares back from the mirror.

And the god replied
*This will be a decisive blow*
*A place that had known decades of fear now had reason to hope*
*we are bringing the war to a responsible end*
*not going to extend this forever war, not extending a forever exit*
*there's a lot of progress made at the beginning, in recent months there*
*has been a resurgence*
*a routine adjustment to achieve the right balance*
*unimpressed by a lack of a whole-of-country, whole-of-government,*
*coherent strategy*

And Odysseus said to her
They call that look your soldiers get
*the thousand yard stare*, but there is no name
for the opposite, the shepherd we left behind
watching me from the airport perimeter,
as the woman about to be stoned stares up at me
from the pit. They have held me
they have captured me
they have given me your last gift
a way of speaking
in layers of ash
the song I make
of what I haven't understood.

And the god answered him
*This document provides clarifying guidance to Discharge Review Boards*
*Our veterans have earned the world-class healthcare*
*value the contribution and sacrifice made by defence members and veterans*
*Since prior diagnoses have been based on the veteran's claim that*
*my Administration has pledged*
*Refrain from giving a diagnosis straight out*
*may be assigned to a priority group if any of the below descriptions are true*
*Appeals withdrawn by applicant 28 per cent of total*

And with that the god closed her empty Kevlar eyes
and dismissed him.

** Translator's note: the god speaks in phrases gleaned from the speeches of Western leaders at the outbreak of wars in Afghanistan and Iraq; and in extracts from official documents produced by veterans' departments in various countries.*

# To those born after a plague year

That you were conceived before the Afterwards of uncommon times
to emerge in such numbers, a 'cohort'
as demographers will call it, in newly-scrubbed wards,
repurposed suites and decommissioned cots
will be your disgrace. At first, your cribbed front lines
will demand nourishment and swaddling
in packed classes of overburdened schools,
hardening to claim a lifetime's coddling
as though born under your own special sign;
and then, you will decamp in droves to whatever forms
and fusions of love your legions compel; then the last jobs
will be divided amongst yourselves, judges presiding eternally in wigs
the same colour as their hair and their face, everlasting gigs
for politicians and celebrities. Last scene of all, any available jabs
for the next plague will go to *your* rest homes, first. As to the coarse
question of what *they* were doing in the lock-down: well, that's another
matter,

of course.

# Treatise on light

Vessels shaped by the light they hold
are given a name
gazelle kidneys Titian
to hold the light, to keep it still long enough
to give us what we have to hold to
carburettor geranium quartz

then Thomas Young opens a window
onto a London morning two centuries ago
and things haven't been the same since. He catches
the light that enters his room and splits it in two
revealing waves that spread out into the invisible
that cross one another forming a disturbance we call
sorrow history desire

now we know those rustling packets we call
God love time
are simply waves playing further out into what
we no longer have a name for
bringing what we have no name for
into the shallows of this world
breaking onto the platform
rolling along the street

waves eddy and collide
interfering with particles that constitute our life
growing stronger as they approach
fate despair memory
simply light bent in different ways

their tug draws us out and down
leaving us, if we're lucky, no more than
perplexed, sensing that something
that lies outside names has passed
still draws us in its wake

but when a wave lifts us
the good days can be so simple:
a pizza shop empty
but for me, my wife and her mother in knitted hats, unwinding scarves
and at another table, a group of joshing pensioners
glass sugar shakers on the plastic menus
catching pewter light
and the pier opposite, extending a runway
for rain announcing itself over the bay.

# The dreamtower

The dreamtower lifts itself towards a night sky
that, like all ceilings, is only there as part of the frame
for all the cavorting that takes place there.
By dint of its hoist, the tower lifts itself above
and out of backyards that you might once have seen from a train
so that, from time to time, you seem to catch a glimpse
of a person you once knew, maybe even someone you loved,
who should, by virtue of their being dead,
not be gesturing at you from some corner of the edifice,
phrases and faces attached like medallions to every angle
on its lattice. Sometimes two people who are beating
one another's faces into bloody meat
make you want to leap from the tower in dismay
as you realise how dispassionately
the surrounding crowd and you are watching
the gruesome suffering that goes on and on.
But then you notice the top of the tower is glinting
in the rising sun's first rays; and if the tower now seems
disjointed, if parts of its frame
seem to be missing
it may be because they're melting away,
just as your recollection tries to follow
the route your dream took
through the streets of concocted cities.
But if your dream offers you one last glimpse
of a row of droplets clinging to a railing —
tiny, translucent moons, their patient trucks of watergrain —
that is enough of a reason for you to realise
the dreamtower is not a crane

does no heavy lifting
and you may wake.

# Netballers in red clay

I'm early, so I sit in the empty stands to watch
a game between kids from a couple of colleges
limbs tanned as red figures on an ancient Greek vase
in relief against an rim of gym bags, indoor soccer nets.
Clay's base reality fills the space between and around
each glance of intent and survey; above them,
darkness lacquers the gym's high ceiling.
With a sheepish grin as he misses for the third time
a goal shooter turns his head away from the play
the way an athlete preparing to launch a discus
turns his head to face the amphora's far handle. Only
this kid's no athlete, his awkward stance reminds me
of our own kids when they were still too young to be sure
of how to let their bodies go into a game,
still learning the rules, hands open at their sides,
determined frowns as if to show they were ready
for the future's feint, swivel, leap, call.

# Moon calendar people

How can they be trusted, whose chief celestial concern
is their favoured world's inconstancy, their hidden half-wafer,
retrieved and ransomed by a child,
open parentheses turned this way and that towards us?
That light's a currency some are driven mad by.
Prudence would assume its influence prevails.
It may be that our worlds circle thus.

What can we make of history written from right to left?
Habitués of what the greater light dispels
they move freely through the past's moonlit rooms
where everything's to be doubted, everything's a reminder
of their laughter that we fear more than their silence,
that faint thumbprint a stubborn parody of the sun's seal.
It may be that our worlds have always circled thus.

Does the moon bleed as it wanes?  Do our daughters
feel its current beneath their skin? Does that stark, drained mask
call from its black frame for our sisters' allegiance,
rending our trust like wisps of cloud across its face?
Does it tug at the hem of Ruth's coat as she labours for them
in fields of corn under the daylight darkness?
It may be that our worlds will always circle thus.

# Astapovo

Here's how I first saw it.

A locomotive, shunted to a side track,
stationary as snow piled onto its running boards
and beside the wheels, drifting in with the twilight;
tracks extending in both directions into
the white expanse. The stationmaster, a silhouette
carrying a tureen from the cottage, steam leaving
a tiny trail that draped itself over the picket fence.
The bed where his lordship lay exactly
like the beds our children slept in years ago,

a single bed against a wall. How many times
did they turn to that wall, as if it were
a screen showing one of those films we used to watch
in the garden, projected onto a sheet; a film
in which they starred in all their hopes and miseries?
I watch as he turns from what I know
must be Anna's face
conjured from his illness, as it appears to him
in the wallpaper. He turns to stare at me
as I peer in at him from the window,
saying nothing
but his eyes saying
*don't come in. Please don't come in*
his troupe saying
*don't go in. You're not to go in*

but the wind, juggling flurries of snow between
streetlight and darkness, saying
*Wait. It will be soon be time.*

# House Red

*Smith's Alternative, Canberra*

Zero degrees. Past the hollow day when words refused to come,
past the last bureaucrats whinging their way home,
chairs being stacked, tables set for tomorrow,
lights being turned off; past a few students who have slipped out for
 takeaway
before returning to their cubicles; past cones of mist
building under Northbourne's white colonnades,
over the chipboard ramp, painted portal to the scuffed chessboard
 linoleum,
past apprentice recluses at opposite ends of the bright red vinyl couches,
arriving at the till, beneath glasses hanging in rows
as though some crystal bovine waits above us to be milked,
light purrs from the glass counter.
My purpose here is almost acquitted: — *waddle it be?* —
—*a glass of your finest, thanks* —
judiciously dispensed from remnants of the last bottle.

Astringency prods the soul awake
to live in the body's moment, don its glands,
put on a coat of such colours as the world might envy
asking '*why have we not been loved as you are loved in your palate?*'
In such recesses epiphany stirs
as if an old muse had emerged from her grotto to demand
a half-remembered comity
to keep her little community alive
teach the tongue its fluency.

# Driving to the conditions

And if travelling even the shortest distance between blank
mesas of 'here' and 'there' is a scrimmage
between what you're meant to feel and the world looking askance
at you – then, before you head off, after everything is packed
and you're making infinitesimal adjustments to the luggage

retreat for a few minutes. Pull a book out at random, read
neither closely nor deeply (the sound of kids being whacked
by one another will prevent that); read
from something that never made it to your virtuous stack
but waited as if certain of your return.
Read just enough to feel that you have tied
one end of a truckies' hitch and pulled it tight

against –what, exactly? That warning stencilled
on the wing mirror that the past is closer than it seems?
Or, from the back seat, the unrelenting rattle
of crockery wandering with no place in the world,
dishes a grandmother loved for their maroon rims,
last vestiges she clung to of a dowry
too rococo now for cohorts who eat food from their laps?
Or the wind that tests every corner of the tarp
as the road climbs into evening's country

your car a hyphen in the road's hard sentence
waved on by solitary windmills, river bights
that turn to check if you're following the immense
salt-stitched, barbed wire bound mud map
and, like the top of a page burned by summer barging

through the blinds, canola's runway lights
guiding you along the continent's illuminated margins.

# Metamorphoses

Mothers never fare well in these stories:

murderers, murdered, lamenting, lamented
deluded, deceived, held in fealty to a regnant logic
or rage that prevails in celestial halls and over the red earth.
Change is instant,
the connection between cause and effect takes place off the page,
as in a dream. One moment a girl's making her way
demurely down some forest path; the next,
she's a laurel or a heifer, tethered and flyblown.
(Nor does she see it coming, she doesn't pause for a moment
at the forest's edge with a presentiment
that she'll no longer be the same on the other side.)
                    Outside these stories,
it's the little changes that matter:
Mum repeats the question she just asked
and there are stories about my childhood and youth
that I know she's made up, that stray further from our truth,
further into villages and suburbs I don't recognise
and can't navigate.
                    Nor do bystanders earn a special role
in those stories, no-one's mystified enough to get a line.
Even the father of the girl can't weep enough
to change her fate. But I keep telling my jokes,
gates in the dam wall raised afresh every day to her delighted laughter.
                    Towards morning
I'm woken by a storm from a dream: I could feel
the skin on my shins growing coarse and dark
its heavy ridges glistening with the pelting rain.

The dream seemed to sense an unkindness
like a kind of sap rising through the heartwood
toward the canopy's astonishment.

# Figure without a landscape

If from the emptiness of space we're surprised to hear
a pod of whales admiring one another's freshly barnacled dorsal fins
and in that photo of us as school chums you've kept on the piano
we're listening to a mountain's chainmail
of crunch and chuckle laid down
as a gravel lane for us to wander
if a stone that we kick to the side of that lane
hums along in its own frequency which, if we could only hear it
we might describe as the sound of something being jettisoned
from the galaxy's tilted dice cup
if even the magpie listening for a worm hears a loamy fidget
beneath its claws, beneath its own sandpapery intent

then why shouldn't absence make its own sound
the sound of its making and of what it was made?

(I hope my absence doesn't sound like change room muzak.)

I watch you place the tone arm onto an LP
from a box you've rescued from the attic
with the solicitude of an aged home companion.
The arpeggio begins its long descent
down the adagio in the Fifth, musicians playing
as the score necessitates and in such sequence
as the audience, not rehearsal, demands,
playing as though they heard the piece as a whole
not in tricky bits, picking up
from this bar or that as infelicities require.

You rummage past Scarpia hearing in his derangement
the worshippers' voices as his own,
two fishermen chatting somewhere.
Tallis's vast water flowing under bridges.

Scrape of a chair. An instrument tocks,
a lark climbs rungs of sunlight.

I'd even settle for something like that cassette tape
we played with such relish on family trips
over and over until it was so stretched
it made the singer's voice wobble predictably,
phrases where the melody wavered
like the scrub on either side we stared at from the back,
blurring past, sometimes fixed for a second, then fixed again
until it seemed bush and melody had become the one thing.

But not this:
not the way you look up at the sound of rafters
contracting in the cold, the way
you seem to be expecting someone to speak
as walls settle for the night
not these coins taped as ballast to weight my tongue
to keep it from skipping, from failing to navigate
the shallow and deep vinyl gorges,
the river between tracks growing wider
merging with the final locked groove at the centre
whispering *da capo, da capo, da capo.*

# By half and by half

*By half and by half again, everything measured is undone.*

The kid on his bike the bike without brakes
by half and by half he is coming down the hill
the officer driving the car with flashing blue lights
isn't interested in the kid on the bike
who by half and by half has narrowly missed the sharp palings
the car with the flashing blue light drives past
by half and by half the kid on the bike
the car with the flashing blue light drives past.

*By half and by half again, everything measured is undone.*
*The arrow won't find its target.*

The woman on her knees in a cell
by half and by half they are coming down the corridor
they can see what has happened to her by half and by half
the officer cradles her head away from the floor
he has carried her by half and by half
he has taken her from her cell down the corridor
to the place where she will be healed
by half and by half she will be healed.

*By half and by half again, everything measured is undone.*
*The arrow won't find its target. The runner never crosses the line first.*

The man who asked for air, by half and by half
he is given twelve breaths. By the nurse
who draws sleep by half and by half from his veins
by the doctor who awakens his heart by half a jolt and by half
by the officer who holds the guards back, by the guards as they stand
back
and slip away by half and by half
by those who judge in half words and half minutes
by his mother waiting half in light half in shadow.

*By half and by half again, everything measured is undone.*
*The arrow won't find its target. The runner never crosses the*
*line first.*
*Every falling grain echoes in the silo.*

# Regan

So there we were, jammed together on the back seat,
Dad in the middle, me and Goneril either side,
holding a hand each when out of the blue
he comes out with that:
'*who's going to look after me?*'
Not '*who loves me the most?*' –
*that* was some childish thing he made up to torment us later.

At first I thought he was joking.
We'd been sitting on the deck in the sunshine,
a good day; all right, I think,
perhaps he's lonely, Mum gone all these years;
and of course Cordelia says nothing, up front,
pretends she's concentrating on the traffic, though I know
she's listening; so I think, yes,
we can put him up for a while,
put up with him for a while,
give him a break till we know what's next.
If I lean back, I can see
the tiniest stratocumulus above us, following the car,
like my dreams just before dawn, the sweetest,
most playful dreams you'll get; never a nightmare, never an angry word,
the kids still young, before their Dad developed his mean streak
before ....

It had nothing to do with the will.
That business started later, when he'd fly into a rage and threaten
to change it; as if his poxy little bungalow
meant anything to any of us; he thought it was his castle

even as it fell to bits around him:
the mould, the mess,
ceilings bruised by every passing storm's fist.

But what could we do? His nights were the worst,
lights on, lights off, kitchen clangour at three.
Many times, awakened myself, I'd go down to find him
peering through the blinds at the empty street
waiting for dawn
mumbling at the cat about the weather
provoked by late night TV's insolent jesting.

Today, I tell myself, it will not matter
if the brand new dressing gown I bought him has disappeared
and I promise myself it will not matter
if his clean clothes and the ones that he's been wearing
form a small mountain on his bed. I say to myself
it will not matter if he greets the food I put before him
with a disappointed grimace. It will not matter if the coffee
we go out for is always too hot and bitter.

'*Are you angry about something*?' he asks me from the sickbed
eyes glinting, not needing to ask, though why or at what –
*of course* the dish I made didn't agree with him,
*of course then* he slept badly all night, and tells me so.

One night, when the pain wakes him, I tell him
'You know, I've made a bed on the couch nearby,
in case you call.' And immediately I regret telling him,
immediately I think: why tell him at all?
Why not show more love in the unannounced act?
Maybe that's what Cordelia sees in the rear view mirror,

but when I looked up at that cloud
beyond the darkness I was circling
as if bound to an orbit that bent me taut
strung as a bow before its release
constantly on patrol, unable to keep my mind off the perimeter
(there's a reason why they put the monsters in the corners of old maps)
not daring to look inwards and so not able to look outwards

when I looked up at that cloud, for once
I felt I no longer knew myself; a stranger,
as one of a group met upon the heath.

# Ode to my black satchel

Some took with them amulets, propped parasols, jade slaves,
some took chariots, infantry, terracotta regiments,
wore torcs, amber beads, lapis lazuli or rope
carried grain, legal tender, crockery and harness
for the journey beyond.
But I would willingly forgo all of these for the black satchel
that slouches in the chair opposite, waiting
until I empty the cup into the pot plant, power down the PC, turn the
  lights off.

It doesn't contain much of value,
other than the prospect that it's possible
to have everything that matters in the afterlife at one's fingertips:
pockets for what I should have said when I was silent,
compartments to separate what was truly important
from what I thought was important,
what I truly wanted from what I told myself I wanted
and, behind a concealed zip, something bulky that seems to weigh
the bag down, as if there were a rock in there; but when I check,
I can only find some old, leaky biros.

Eternity must sound like the interior of an overnight Greyhound bus:
years going by like the highway's broken lines outside,
the intermittent interrogations of zippers
opening and closing forever in the darkness
while I grope for these familiar handles,
twisted until they're almost inside out
but still, with the kindness of a fellow-passenger,
fitting comfortably in my palm,

my rummaging a promise
to accompany this object on its journey
as it attends to me on mine.

# Hilarious contraption

*Yves Klein, 'Leap Into the Void', 1960*

The picture shows a man leaping from a second-floor window. It doesn't seem too high to land without injury, if he jumps feet first. But that exuberant swan dive, head up, arms outstretched, defies gravity the way some carnivals have people jump off piers in hilarious contraptions: gliders, bicycles, bathtubs, cartons. He has the same beatific expression as those contestants before they hit the water. Formal shirt cuffs suggest ceremony rather than stunt. Some months before this photo was taken, in the same neighbourhood, my father found lodgings in a house where the landlady asked her tenants kindly not to commit suicide by leaping from the windows. These days, of course, we prefer to see the second photograph, the one that makes it happen, that denies the void. Eight men straining to hold a tarpaulin taut, a photographer crouched beside them focused on the falling figure. The man on the bicycle — who will appear to be riding by in the first photograph, like the ship in Bruegel's *Icarus* — is circling nearby to await his turn.

## Solstice

All done for the day' the machine pronounces cheerfully.
No more meetings, ads, gripes
(I've been ghosted by the future)
But it's a chance for us to head out

my daughter and I stop for provisions as the lights blink on
in the supermarket, where a single worker greets us.
Hummocks of the homeless still in the doorway.
Early communion queue for coffee; pre-schoolers on their way
to the rivers of Babylon; a row of faces at the bus stop lit by little screens.
Beloved morning that brings me a town to admire.

She takes the corners fast on the short drive down the valley
to just below the dam where she and her brother used to cross the weir
barefoot. Crossing these days would be out of the question
as the slipway draws spray like a magician's sleight of hand
across the creek, now in full spate; though she's still without socks,
a gesture of defiance at her pleasure in being out
in the freezing mountain air.

On the drive down, I'm thinking of tales about women
who descend into realms of darkness; how these stories shed details
as if deflecting embers of anger that flitter upwards
in the air's dim chimneys. They don't tell us
what those who stood by and watched
while a young woman walked down a path into deepening shade
might have felt after she disappeared; or even how they got there,
how they prepared, how those who had accompanied her felt
on the walk back
— the stories are silent.

Nor do they tell us whether, when these women reappear,
when they relinquish the darkness, with hope, or regret,
perhaps congratulate themselves on their narrow escape,
on the intensity with which they can now see in the daylight,
they might also look back to wonder how on that day, at that time,
they could have followed such an unsatisfactory path
to an imagined destination. The stories are silent
because nobody can remember back that far,
to our first language in the memories we create for someone else.

I try to take a selfie with her but I can see that she has placed herself
out of the picture. In my clumsy attempt to frame us,
I have caught only a tilted avenue of poplars.
We follow the path above the creek to the dam lookout.
Some signs are still scorched by the fires of two decades ago,
as if the earth remembers pain, as if the wild places and the tamed
are scarred by what happened, still needing to say something
about what occurred in that place.
I'm trying to ignore the cold, but the path is steep
and slow going, the creek following below us
a flow of incidents catching the light.

In the end, bystanders have to accept that their place in the story
is to be the bystander
witnesses must agree to be witnesses
the chorus has to wait in the wings for a chance
to perfect its job; which is to wait,
wanting only to be astonished
by astonishingly ordinary days
to share the commonplace creations
all done for the day.

# The sadness of traditional instruments

is because they yearn to go back
to return to where they were once played
before the big stage
before the big audience
the kore can smell the earth after rain on the edges of the forest
the shamisen is listening to the village turning in for the night
what they sang before the words were added
what they sang before the songs were famous
they pay close attention to what surrounds them
because they are unhomed
the charango dreams of clouds hiding the distant peaks
the sarod is on a bus heading home
from the market with three women
who sold nothing
but make each other laugh
the santuri has stopped for a drink
men playing cards in a lozenge of light
notes like tobacco brushed off a knee
coloured lanterns moving in the freshening wind
how can we hear that

# Ghost story

Coming into the room, it's easy to see where to start. He packs
his old records away: with no machine to play them on
he can't listen to them anyway. While he's at it,
he strips his shelves bare of books he knows he'll never read,
his eyes too tired these days to cope with tiny fonts.

He sweeps away old knick-knacks he had kept for no reason
other than the effort to get rid of them. Watches weather from snowdomes
melt into the carpet's patterns, consigns his clothes
to the charity bins; they no longer fit,
they reek with the incense of experience.

He closes his windows to the clatter of milk crates from the street downstairs,
to the unruliness of coffee and, when the breeze is being unkind, the sea.
He begins to forget the name of friends he let go long ago,
makes a small bonfire of diaries he kept in failing boxes, letters from a past
he no longer recognises. And now, since he's lost his touch

he no longer needs the future: the table
that honours his hunger is spread before him

he no longer needs his home: rooms he once yearned
to come back to that no longer seem to welcome him

he no longer needs his love, its walls blown away by wind or war
his soul left exposed like furniture to the onlookers below

he no longer needs his voice, a pale gulch rustling
with names that fill his mouth with stones

he has no more need for his body, that scuffed suitcase
left to circle on the days' carousel.

The haunting is complete. He goes outside. It's morning
in streets where he has arrived for the first time.
They don't see him, ask nothing of him. They're waiting so

he steps out of his skin
            and steps free
                        steps out
                                    steps beyond

# Bright square of morning

Leaving Melbourne, the highway curves slowly past estates
shoaling into paddocks and foothills
as if half-inclined to take one last look back
        at the hazy city.
If you leave early enough,
                just at that bend,
        in a line to the distance the road would have followed if it hadn't
          turned away,

your eye will be drawn to the side of a large shed
        shining in the dawn; so radiant
that this blank, yellow square is its own light source,
        the very point
from which the morning is unfurling.

As the day's distances begin
        and dozing passengers give you time to think
about another set of appointments kept, opportunities missed,
        this shape offers just enough distraction
to blunt that retinue's claim until
                it falls behind
with the B-double convoys dispersing
        into the fat quarters of the interior.

For a moment held by a line of sight, that immanent light
        seems to offer something more than the kilometres to come
of dishevelled bottlebrush, cable railings
        squaring the gravel verge
adolescent cliques of skewed gum saplings

the brightness of that wall is like a page
        behind which a torch is shining
        revealing the page's opalescent swash,
a trace of the crush and scrape that brings paper out of water
        as though something of a sapling's leap toward
the sun is echoèd in light's flecks and fibres
as if the writing across its face
        is the least important thing.

# Kafka's Children

Franz, you do not have the right
you do not have the right to take them with you
even if you begged for it        as you demanded it
in your will        in your signed and legal hand
in a contract        watermarked and imprinted
in an envelope        sealed by a dying man's tongue
tell me which nation tendered this right
in which plenum was it voted
show me the names of those who signed
explain with what currency they paid for it
this is no longer your story to tell
Franz, pity the correspondence
pity the correspondents
they still join their claim
still make their plea
from the queue at the airport
the plane is about to leave
Oxfords gleaming
your Homburg impeccable
you have grasped them by the scruff
the ungainly
the awkward
they stumble in their haste
as you force them across the tarmac
yet they are still speaking to you hopefully
even now        even as they disappear
into the future's cold blue air

## Landing lights

Above trees I can see through the kitchen window
that over the years my parents have lived here
have grown just tall enough to hide the sea

I'm watching a bright light that appears from time to time
a brilliant planet that seems to hang over borderlands
of tussock and thistle on the bay's western side.

While I'm preparing their dinner, my wife remains over there
where I imagine her unpicking a mistake
she's made in her quilt because she's tired

and I wish I could be over there too, telling her to leave it; I would tell her
about how the Navajo stitch a tiny line into their rugs
to show a weaver's soul the way to leave the work and rejoin the world.

That light seems to hover for a few moments, and then
as if it's made a decision veers away and vanishes
until it reappears a few minutes later.

It took me a while to realise it's only the main flight path into the city
that briefly positions planes to face us
shining into this room where Mum's sitting before the TV

appalled, in the dark, because she's seeing again, in her lifetime,
the aged, the sick, spreadeagled between mattresses, cots,
a few pots and a chair piled onto carts

pulled by their sons along the ruts, through ruined villages
across lands and histories loved and cursed by their unhappy tribes
into open fields of twilight beneath inexplicable lights.

# On the morning my daughter leaves

blue- and gold-fringed morning cloud sees her off
as always; as always, cattle preside
at their stolid desks beside the road
where it nestles into the curve of the river,
sleep dazzling her with its headlights in the mirror.
      So now she has gone
out, entered that municipality of potential
from where she emerges into lights at the service station,
the queue at the bakery, walking past mulchy rose beds
with their retinue of courtiers in rice-paddy hats.
I imagine the steps she is taking *one at a time*
as always, as advised, *one foot in front of the other*,
becoming a stride, wider and wider
until, as one loved by the ground over which she soars,
she is given flight by joy,
embraced by air-lilt, wispstream.
      A character from the classics
in a box on the back seat,
she crests a hill, surveys the town still sleeping under dawn,
first rays touching its spires, steeples,
the weathervanes with metal roosters
making real cries, walls round its locked courtyards wet with dew,
shining like the jewelled breastplates of the distant windows,
the horizon opens its arms
and she is welcomed to the vanishing point.

# Poem written in deep blue

*the quest for the imagination/must be begun all over again*
— Zbigniew Herbert

Machines these days produce poetry of such beauty
even the chimpanzees writing Hamlet have to pause in admiration.
Algorithms decide the best match of wheelbarrows and rain
learn how to play tennis without a net
in imaginary gardens with real toads (but no bugs)
effortlessly recapture emotion in tranquil lines of code
that resist normality almost successfully.
Every day programmers die miserably
for systems that make nothing happen.
Even the algorithms are poetry. Words made out of machines,
spreadsheets with formulas for ranking
doubts and mysteries in one column,
facts and reasons in another.
I give up.
I go to the family room where the TV is on
showing a couple of kids from China
competing in a figure skating championship.
They move with such grace, together,
they make one creature that slides alone
through its own element: part-dream,
part-water, part-memory, giving itself
to the white landscape of its joy
oblivious
to how it will be caught
by one finger
that touches the ice.

# Yellow on yellow

In her wide-open sanctuary
a female sun moth's yellow patches are hard to spot
as she lies against grasses allowed to fend for themselves
in baking-paper paddocks, you and I circling
their deliberate rendition, these hardly promising
*'coarsely vesicular, minor interbedded silty sand and baked soils'*
of the city's far western edge, under a gathered sky
solar ringbolt at its centre. Herons heading for the wetlands
seem to give this place a wide berth.
Everything lies low:
tumbleweed mustard, daisy, details of the plain's wider story,
stellar scumble of oxalis.
It would be easy, I suppose, to hold a suburb in contempt
thrown together in its sameness like a child's clutch of sand
but a woman in a brilliant sari is taking her grandchild to a playground
where New Holland honeyeaters are comparing their tiny golden
epaulettes.

# Library at night

Waiting for my wife to end her late shift at the desk,
I see the shelves are full these days; the books are always
there now, ready to be found: right shelf, right sequence,
no longer misplaced by error or design. On the bottom shelf
books genuflect, spines kowtow; those on the top stare outwards
with optimism and bravado. English Lit on Level Three
rustles with assiduous highlights, diffident question marks
as though one of the Lake Poets sitting above the mist
had come in to make some notes. A level up,
it's much noisier around 320 to 329, where Pol Sci
reverberates with furious denunciations in biro,
exclamation marks and slogans declaiming from the margins.

A sweet scent of acid lingers,
as if all those authors were waiting somewhere
in the darkened upper floors, wearing
an old-fashioned cologne: '*Eau des Livres*', or '*Parfum des Cahiers*'.
Dog-eared paperbacks, textbooks with huge sans serif titles
bisected by gaudy geometric planes, or still older books
with green and gold embossed boards, backstrips with a tiny emblem,
gilt fore-edge, colophons' triumphal arch,
many still with borrowing slips stuck inside the back
displaying check-out dates from when books were carried
in teetering columns of aspiration
to the loans desk where, before being stamped,
each one was turned over, considered,
commented on, as if being fussed over
and tucked in for its long journey.

I still check them out, to give them one last read,
one last opportunity to show how hard they'd worked
to offer what they had:
impossibly old-fashioned, quaint, unmoored certainties,
portly courtesies, paragraphs tooled and toiled over,
the one felicitous phrase
that I will go searching for years hence
as it flashes in my memory
the way an antique brooch momentarily catches the sunlight.

# A short history of writing

In the morning, I went out with the officials.
We kept our characters thick and clear
adopting the peremptory voice
so that every citizen in the villages and towns we came to
could understand the rules.
Our decrees were affixed to mileposts
and tavern walls, edicts at eye level.
Truly 'top down', as they say.
With a seal embossed with the sign for fire,
nobody could fail to understand the consequences
of disobedience.

In the afternoon, I sat with the scholars.
We sought beauty for our calligraphy.
It merged and overlapped, eddied and meandered
adopting a melodious voice
for this scroll as it draped across our knees,
unrolled across courtyards and town squares.
People hurried past on their errands,
occasionally stopping to lift a corner.
After much bickering, the seal was imprinted
with the sign for air,
so everyone would understand it was impossible
to divide the scroll into parts.

In the evening, rain dissolved my paper.
My resolution weakened by the twilight,
I was beset by doubts about whether I had anything to say,
what voice was left for me to say it in,

who would stand in the downpour to read it?
My brushes were dishevelled, and as the characters ran and blotted,
they ended up making words I hadn't intended.
I have no seal, but I stamped the fragments anyway,
with the sign for earth, as if to say:
Here. This, too, has its place.

# Re:Vision

BRAHMS PIANO TRIO NO 1 OP 8
COMPOSED 1854, REVISED 1889

He tells Clara 'It will not be as wild as before',
but keeps both scores to show her what's changed.
She reminds him he signed the first one with a nickname. He explains
it's because he liked the way it suggested a body
in orbit, wandering; I imagine him adding coyly
(after all, he was only 20 at the time, and Clara
was already alone by then) that perhaps he meant
gravity as someone else's influence?

I'm listening to the second version as I stroll
before returning to the office for the afternoon where they
will tell me
I'm going to lose my job.
Sometimes a piece of music, a needle-drop, accompanies your life so well
it becomes the sound of your thinking.
Or perhaps it's the life, once or twice a decade,
that catches up with the score,
the key that harmonises a life and its work.

My reverie roams the same span of years
as elapsed between his first and second versions.
It seemed to him then that life would move forward in the form of a trio:
exposition,
development,
recapitulation.
But early reviews were ambiguous:
*'Very enterprising, very adventurous, very self-confident...'*

Then time sped up, things
had to be said more clearly, more simply, or simply
make their claim to be said at all.
So some themes never come back fully, they head off
in different directions, different instruments, different years
as if that first iteration were naïve; the second version
looks at the first with affection, sympathy,
that person not quite a stranger,
a chance to reconcile with the younger man.
Not an older man giving advice to his younger self,
but a chance to hear the younger man
giving an account
of himself to the one he will become.
Revision remakes a life, offers possibility
through the choices redaction demands
between what is to be remembered or put aside,
kept or discarded.

Clara's presence is what links the two versions,
the years of their life together
and apart, because there is no part of the revision
that is not a question about what might, what should, what did
or couldn't. He watches as she pores
over a manuscript. How grey her hair has become.
They have spent a lifetime together.
Forever unfinished,
forever three of them, a trio, even one who leaves
early. Different instruments prevail –
– violin the bright current of yearning
cello the dark gold of resignation –
but always an undercurrent of what she has held back,
hidden from his sight and understanding.

That crescendo as the first movement ends
is the soundtrack to the last days of an empire.
(My century is only eleven years away.)
I join men in waistcoats
smoking cigars at their desks,
whispering the talismanic names of high officials
whose moods and views are carefully assessed
as they pass down the corridors between partitions
swinging simple gym bags as marks of their rank
that contrast with my eager, shiny briefcase,
expandable for work to take home. Choristers and
fusiliers
display popular cartoons on their cravats.
Sometimes duels are fought. But I'm ready for what comes next.
*Allegro con brio.*

# Acknowledgements & Notes

Grateful acknowledgement is made to the editors of the following publications and websites in which a number of these poems first appeared:

*Antipodes; Australian Catholic University Poetry Prize 2022; Avalon Literary Review; Be:longing; Island; Last Stanza; Meniscus; Nostos; New York Quarterly; Panorama: The Journal of Travel, Place, and Nature; Poetica; P76 (Rochford Street Review); Quadrant; Slant; Southword; StylusLit; Westerly.*

My thanks to the judges and editors who selected the following poems (or versions of them):

'Pumping Station' appeared in *Best of Australian Poems 2022;* 'And who among the angels' was awarded the Yeats Poetry Australia Prize 2022; 'Ode to my Black Satchel' was awarded the Letter Review Prize for Poetry; 'The sadness of traditional musical instruments' was commended in the Melbourne Poets Union International Poetry Prize 2022, and 'Astapovo' was shortlisted for the MPU Prize in 2023; 'There's some mighty good water in Tennessee' was shortlisted for the Atlanta Review International Poetry Prize 2022; 'Treatise on Light' was shortlisted for the 2022 Bridport Prize. 'Figure without a landscape' was shortlisted for the 2023 Tom Collins Poetry Prize. 'The Tidbinbilla Plates', 'The museum of unmet expectations' and 'On the origins of the empirical method' were awarded first, second and highly commended in the 29th Melbourne Poets Union International Poetry Prize 2024; 'Landing Lights' was highly commended in the 2024 Fellowship of Australian Writers (WA) Tom Collins Prize. 'Fricatives of the Western Wood Peewee' was highly commended in the 2024 Rialto Nature and Place Poetry Competition.

Thank you, Amanda and Penelope, for the close reading and support reflected in your comments on the cover.

My thanks as always to Ross Gillett for his incisive and supportive editorial comments and to Dave Musgrave at Puncher & Wattmann for this publication.

Source for the italicised line in 'Yellow on yellow', p 76: Vandenberg AHM, 1974, 'Melbourne: Geological Survey of Victoria', Mines Department Melbourne Victoria, http://epbcnotices.environment.gov.au/_entity/annotation/eee475b1-7c8f-ec11-80d1-00505684c137/a71d58ad-4cba-48b6-8dab-f3091fc31cd5?t=1645053126398

www.ingramcontent.com/pod-product-compliance
Ingram Content Group Australia Pty Ltd
76 Discovery Rd, Dandenong South VIC 3175, AU
AUHW020951120325
408206AU00001B/5

9 781923 099418